WINSLOW HOMER 1836-1910

A Selection from the Cooper-Hewitt Collection, Smithsonian Institution

Published for the Cooper-Hewitt Museum of Decorative Arts and Design, Smithsonian Institution
by the SMITHSONIAN INSTITUTION PRESS   City of Washington   1972

Library of Congress Catalog Card Number 72-1527

For sale by the Superintendent of Documents
United States Government Printing Office
Washington, D. C. 20402 – Price $3.00
Stock number 4703-0014

CONTENTS

FOREWORD

Whenever drawings from the Cooper-Hewitt Collections are discussed, words of wonder and gratitude leap to mind for those indefatigable and enthusiastic Hewitt sisters, the granddaughters of Peter Cooper. It was they who assumed the responsibility of establishing, on the fourth floor of the Cooper Union, the museum intended by their visionary grandfather. Limitations of space influenced the Hewitts to restrict the scope of the collections to no later than the first quarter of the nineteenth century. The stairwells of the building, however, were considered independently, as Peter Cooper had specified that these walls be lined with objects of interest to the ascending and descending students. Not long after the museum's founding in 1896, the corridors and staircases were adorned with works of late nineteenth- and early twentieth-century American artists such as Frederic E. Church, Robert Blum, and Winslow Homer.

In addition to their own energetic activity on behalf of the museum, Eleanor and Sarah Hewitt were highly successful in transmitting their enormous enthusiasm for the project to their friends and acquaintances, among whom were Mr. and Mrs. Charles Savage Homer, Jr., Winslow's brother and sister-in-law. To the Homers' generous gifts of drawings and paintings were added in due course other donations of drawings, along with a nearly complete series of wood engravings by the artist.

Many of the works have been seen before (the *Young Soldier* is the most frequently reproduced picture in the

museum's collection), but some of the drawings are
published here for the first time. They have been studied
and discussed by students of Winslow Homer and, in
particular, by Lloyd Goodrich, whose notes of thirty years,
along with his encouragement, interest, and knowledge of
Homer — freely shared — made a major contribution to this
catalog.

   We are deeply grateful to John Wilmerding for his essay,
"Winslow Homer's Drawings." Elaine Evans Dee and
Xenia Cage of the Department of Drawings and Prints, have
been involved in all stages of the catalog.

LISA TAYLOR, *Director*
Cooper-Hewitt Museum of Decorative Arts and Design

INTRODUCTION

The Cooper-Hewitt Museum's collection of paintings, drawings, and watercolors by Winslow Homer is one of the most complete representations of a nineteenth-century American artist in any museum. The drawings in particular, numbering several hundred, cover every stage of Homer's long career, and most aspects of his wide range of subjects. They form a unique record of the evolution of a major artist. The oils are the largest group of his early paintings in any institution.

After Winslow Homer's death in 1910, almost three-hundred drawings were found in his studio at Prout's Neck, Maine. (As many more, according to his family, had been destroyed by mice.) In 1912 his elder brother, Charles Savage Homer, Jr., who had always been especially close to him, gave the drawings and some watercolors to the Cooper Union Museum for the Arts of Decoration. This generous gift was augmented within a few years by a group of paintings, making a total gift of 272 drawings, twenty-two oils, one oil sketch, and fourteen watercolors. In 1916 two more drawings, including the fine *Herring Net*, were given by Charles W. Gould, a trustee of the museum, a friend of Homer's, and a leading collector of his works.

Winslow Homer began his career as an artist in black and white: a lithographer, then an illustrator. From his youth, he drew constantly. Not until he was almost twenty-seven did he begin to paint seriously. All of his pictures, including his most painterly mature oils and watercolors, were built on a basis of strong draftsmanship. His drawings from the first showed a sure grasp of action and character, graphic skill, largeness of form, broad massing of lights and shadows, an instinctive sense of decorative pattern.

Homer's drawings are a kind of visual autobiography, revealing the many varied aspects of the contemporary scene that interested him: life in and around Boston before he came to New York; the Civil War, in camp and on the battlefield; country life in fashionable summer resorts and on the farm; childhood in the country; the hardy English fisherfolk of Tynemouth on the North Sea, where he spent two seasons in 1881 and 1882 — a turning point in his career; and finally the seacoast of Maine, his solitary home for his last twenty-seven years.

Homer's drawings in his early career as an illustrator and reportorial artist were obviously done on the spot, from life. They were raw material for his finished illustrations and paintings. This does not detract from their artistic quality — on the contrary. Then, in the 1870's, after he stopped illustrating, he began to produce more drawings that were intended as works of art in themselves, such as the delightful 1878-1879 series featuring country boys and girls, combining first-hand observation and unsentimental idyllicism; the strong Tynemouth scenes with their constant sense of the perils of the sea; and the masterly studies of the rugged weatherbeaten shore of Prout's Neck. That Homer thought of such drawings as independent works of art is proved by the fact that he exhibited them frequently and held several exhibitions of drawings only.

Also among the Cooper-Hewitt drawings are a number of studies for paintings, including some tantalizing ones for pictures that he never executed. Homer was always reticent about his methods of creation, like everything of a personal nature, so that we know comparatively little about how his paintings were composed. These studies, however, seem to indicate that he did not customarily make detailed preliminary drawings, but drew broad sketches of the motif, and that he probably worked out the composition in his mind, and then on canvas.

All the oils in the Cooper-Hewitt collection (except one Civil War study) belong to the late 1860s and the 1870s, and therefore do not represent the major breakthrough in his art that Homer achieved after he settled in Maine. Their general subject matter is his favorite one in those years — country life: the changing seasons, comely young ladies seen outdoors, the simpler world of the farm, the pleasures of rural childhood. Mostly modest in scale, sometimes not entirely finished, these paintings have in common the freshness of eye, the skill of hand, and the utter authenticity that marked Homer's work all of his life.

LLOYD GOODRICH, *Consultant*
Whitney Museum of American Art

WINSLOW HOMER'S DRAWINGS

The occasion of an exhibition of drawings by a major artist is important and useful in several ways. We are afforded the opportunity of looking over the artist's shoulder, so to speak, to observe him at work. In some instances when there are a number of preparatory studies for one work, we can examine the creative process unfolding as the evolution of an idea moves from its germination to final resolution. The fact that Winslow Homer developed, modified, and deepened certain central themes throughout his career lends additional interest. Because he is a major figure in the history of American art, such an exhibition helps to illuminate further our understanding of the nature of American painting in the nineteenth century. A relatively neglected area of his creative achievement, these drawings have a special appeal both as preliminary sketches—often for important oils—and as vigorous visual statements with an artistic quality all their own.

As is quickly evident, Homer worked in a variety of media and styles when making his sketches. Many of his drawings are in pencil, but he also made use of pen, charcoal, and chalk. Occasionally, he used a colored paper (tan, blue, green) besides the usual white to capture special effects of water or atmosphere. His manner of drawing likewise varies from hasty, impulsive notations to careful, clear outlines and details. Sometimes he only sought to catch the contours and posture of a figure; in other instances, he attempted to suggest the mood or character of weather; and, in still other cases, he used his drawings to begin working out the relationships between forms or some sense of a total compositional structure.

Because a substantial bibliography on Homer already exists, added to in recent years by specialized studies of different periods or facets of his career, we probably have now most of the salient facts of his biography and a clear general view of his stylistic development. Every Homer biographer has had to begin and end with the painter's cultivated reticence and guarded seclusion. To William Howe Downes, who requested information from the artist during his lifetime for a book on his life and art, Homer replied that "the most interesting part of my life is of no concern to the public," and declined to furnish him with any help. In his own way, Homer is telling us that we should scrutinize his art for the revelations of his life, the expressions of his innermost feelings and ideas. His forceful and memorable pictures ultimately become the "most interesting part" of his life. We are fortunate to have a large group of drawings which together reveal something of the ways in which the artist conceived and nurtured his responses to humanity and the natural world.

Included in the Cooper-Hewitt group are sketches from almost every phase of Homer's career. In subject, they range from the lighthearted to the profoundly serious. They illustrate both his debt to other artists and his own originality and inventiveness. Among the earliest items in the collection is the 1855 watercolor drawing of *Setting a Squirrel Trap*. A youthful work done at the time that Homer was an apprentice in John W. Bufford's lithography shop in Boston, it suggests that he had become aware of the work of older American genre artists like David Claypoole Johnson and William Sidney Mount. Johnson had preceded Homer by a decade or so as a music-sheet illustrator in the same Boston firm, and one finds clear echoes of the older artist's caricatured and gesturing figures in Homer's own music-sheet illustrations. In addition, engravings after the work of Mount and George Caleb Bingham were circulating widely through the American Art-Union and other institutions at this time. This early drawing of two youths setting their trap especially recalls Mount's painting *The Dead Fall* or *Trap Sprung* of 1844 and the related *Catching Rabbits* of 1893 (both in the Suffolk Museum, Stony Brook, New York) which was engraved about 1850. Whether or not explicitly derived from such a source, Homer's celebration of youth and the out-of-doors has its firm base in the traditions of American art flourishing by the middle decades of the century.

There is a strong group of Civil War sketches. Some, like those of cavalry soldiers on horseback, show how close Homer's style came at this time to Eastman Johnson — for example, *The Wounded Drummer Boy*, 1871, in the Union League Club of New York. Johnson also saw action at the front; he knew and worked near Homer in the University Studio Building in New York after the war. If there is a distinction between the two, one senses a greater energy pulsating through Homer's lines as he delineates a figure.

Other drawings reflect an interest simply in recording a head or figure from several different points of view or in related poses. Clearly these were notations which he might use later in the preparation of a wood engraving for *Harper's Weekly* magazine or for a more ambitious oil painting, a medium he was just taking up at this point. Still other images from the war have a distinct seriousness and poignance of their own. An example is the *Wounded Soldier Being Given a Drink from a Canteen.* Part of the power in Homer's observation is the close-up point of view and the isolation of the figures in strong patterns against the page. The drawing has a stark, laconic quality similar to his best known *Harper's* illustration from this period, *The Sharpshooter.* Both suggest that Homer may well have been aware of the other major form of visual illustration of the Civil War, namely photography. The unsentimental and objective realism, the forms occasionally cropped at the framing edges of the page, and the sense of two-dimensional pattern are close in spirit and vision to the striking photographs being taken at this time by Mathew Brady, Timothy O'Sullivan, and Alexander Gardner. There are, of course, other parallels to the new realism in the Civil War fiction of Stephen Crane, most notably his *Red Badge of Courage*, and the poetry of Walt Whitman, who also had first hand experience of the war's brutality. Together, this generation of artists was creating new modes of expression. If anything, the Civil War made them, and Homer especially, aware both of man's humanity and his mortality.

If his experience at the front and his work for *Harper's* might possibly have introduced Homer to the language of photography, he certainly knew of it a few years later when he went abroad. One of his few pictures from the Paris trip of 1866-1867, *The Gargoyles of Notre Dame* (collection James M. Thomson) was based directly on an 1851 calotype by Charles Negre of *Henry Le Secq at Notre Dame Cathedral* (collection Andre Jammes, Paris). Related to this, either as a preliminary study or as a humorous variation, is Homer's drawing *View of Paris.* With the rooftops below, a man leans out over the railing extending a wishbone to tempt back a cat crouched at the end of a stone gargoyle. The absurdity of the situation and the staring expressions of man, animal, and stone face produce a comic touch uncommon in Homer's work.

Also probably related to the Paris trip is the unusual drawing *International Tea Party*, thought to date from a few years later when Homer made two illustrations for *Harper's* on this subject. The obvious Oriental figures and flat patterning of forms indicate the likelihood of Homer's exposure to Japanese prints as well as to contemporary French painting during his stay in Paris. The relaxed, seated figures, especially the rather fashionable women, recall pictures such as Manet's *Garden of the Tuileries* of 1860-1862, Monet's *Terasse a St. Addresse* of 1866, and the early café scenes by Renoir.

After returning from Paris, Homer set about recording

life in America as it readjusted itself to peacetime pursuits and leisures. Fashionable resorts like Long Branch, New Jersey, drew his attention, as did increasingly the country-side of the White Mountains in New Hampshire and the shoreline of Gloucester, Massachusetts. A favorite topic of these years was youth, and among the Cooper-Hewitt drawings is a small, crisp study for one of Homer's best known oils from this period, *Snap the Whip*. The group of boys is more tightly interlocked here than they are in the finished painting (Butler Institute, Youngstown, Ohio). Homer spread out the figures more laterally across the final composition, allowing for greater clarity of each figure and rhythmic play of silhouette among them. Like its companion *Breezing Up* a few years later, *Snap the Whip* is ultimately an image of sheer joy and optimism. It is again close in style and feeling to Eastman Johnson's work; his *Old Stage Coach* (Milwaukee Art Center) was painted the year before and may well have influenced Homer's own conception. Another associate of both men in New York was the genre painter Enoch Wood Perry, who also painted a picture similar to these, *The Pemigewisset Coach* (Shelburne Museum).

The theme of boys having fun was a popular one in American art and literature at this time. Such youths became projections of a comic abandon and naive truthful-ness that seemed missing in the adult Victorian world of the brown decades. They are the heroes of stories by Charles Dudley Warner and Mark Twain; it is significant that

Huckleberry Finn was published in the same year that Homer painted *Breezing Up*. These works were by artists concerned on the surface with humor, but beneath with serious truths. As such, they tell us something about American life during the Grant era as well as something more profound about the human condition. Homer see the joy, innocence, and honesty of childhood as characteristics of humanity — characteristics that do not have to disappear when youth passes into age.

Homer's second trip abroad, to Tynemouth, England, in 1881-1882, was a major turning point in his career. His subjects thereafter were more serious, and he took up new media as well. He now developed watercolor as expressive in its own right, no longer a form of a colored drawing preparatory to an oil painting. The confrontation of man and nature becomes a recurrent theme. From this time on, human will, endurance, and survival are the central subjects of his oils, watercolors, and drawings. An evocative example is *Two Women and a Child at a Rail, Tynemouth*, one of a series that depicts these figures watching a storm. From the various pen and pencil sketches first came a watercolor and an etching, then an oil *Coming Away of the Gale* in 1883, which Homer finally reworked a decade later as *Gale* (Worcester Art Museum). Frequently, in these drawings and paintings his figures are isolated and anon-ymous, set against the forces of nature or engaged in the hard labors of making a living (see the study for *The Herring Net*).

After Tynemouth, Homer's techniques also changed. His watercolors are more somber and fluid, more economical and expressive. In subject and execution, they suggest a new strength and gravity. During the eighties he also took up etching and charcoal, both of which allowed him to capture atmospheric effects more readily. Often there is a foreboding note in his work, as in the *Shore with Clouded Sky* done in charcoal, with its small figure running across the foreground before the storm. More characteristically, his subjects intimated tragedy, its possibility as well as the human drama of overcoming it. *The Life Line* of 1884 was but one in a series of major canvases through Homer's later years dealing with man's tenuous but heroic mortality. In the drawing for this work, he delineates the features of both figures carefully if generally; with the subsequent oil, he made the important change of having the woman's scarf blow across her rescuer's face, thus creating an anonymity that is both immediate and universal. From the beginning Homer has joined male and female together, interlocking them with a complex tangle of limbs. His final design was stark and monumental in its isolation of the figures against the background of treacherous breakers. The pattern of contrasting forms in the drawing took on a powerful abstraction as Homer proceeded, until in the end it became both an image and a metaphor of oppositions, between life and lifelessness, action and inertia, ship and shore, man and nature.

During the nineties, Homer seemed to be summarizing types and themes first taken up a decade or two before, deepening and clarifying their meaning with each new version. Often the ideas in one picture overlapped with others conceived or underway at the same time. For example, the studies for *The Lookout—"All's Well"* also anticipated *The Wreck*, both done in 1896. In the latter, the figure of a man clad in oilskins strides across the dunes waving. Is he calling for further assistance or simply drawing attention to the wreck on the other side of the ledge? The man waving here is a reworking of the figure in *The Lookout*. The drawings show us the variations in which an arm was to be raised, the precise expression of the mouth calling—in one instance a cry of reassurance, in the other of disaster—and how the sou'wester was to frame the head. Homer's struggle is to find both a realism and an abstraction that will most forcefully express his meaning. This was equally true of his great contemporary in American literature, Herman Melville.

The physical and the metaphysical presence of nature increasingly became Homer's subjects in his last years. In the end, he unveiled the humanity of nature itself. Man individually may not be present in many of his later works, but his presence is nonetheless felt. Looking at the nature studies and the great landscapes of Homer's later career, one is reminded of his central place in the nineteenth century, a century so concerned with geology and establishing the age of the earth. This was also a period that produced Charles Darwin and his search for the origin of species.

These parallel interests in the evolution of man and his environment receive fitting visual expression in Homer's mature art, which holds the human and natural worlds in such heroic balance.

JOHN WILMERDING, *Chairman*
Department of Art, Dartmouth College

CATALOG OF THE EXHIBITION

Prepared by

ELAINE EVANS DEE
Curator of Drawings and Prints
Cooper-Hewitt Collections

Except for two drawings identified as given by
Charles W. Gould, all drawings and paintings were the
gift of Mr. and Mrs. Charles Savage Homer, Jr.

Dimensions are in inches and parenthetically
in millimeters; height precedes width

Drawings

1.

SETTING A SQUIRREL TRAP
 About 1855
 Study for the wood engraving, "Christmas—Gathering
 Evergreens," *Harper's Weekly*, December 25, 1858
 Pencil, green, brown and gray wash; $8^{5}/_{16}$ x $11\frac{1}{2}$
 (211 x 292)
 1912-12-268

2.

COWS IN A PASTURE
   About 1855
   Study for an illustration in *The Song of the Sower* by
   William Cullen Bryant, New York, 1871, p. 19
   Pencil, watercolor; 5⁷/₁₆ x 8¹¹/₁₆
   (139 x 221)
   1912-12-52

3.

HOUSE WITH A PORCH

About 1860
Pencil, blue, red, and brown wash on brown paper; 7 x 10
(177 x 254)
1912-12-267

4.

GENERAL McCLELLAN'S SIXTH CAVALRY
REGIMENT, EMBARKING AT ALEXANDRIA FOR
OLD POINT COMFORT

1862

Study for an illustration in "McClellan at the Head of the
Grand Army; Recollections of a Private — VII," by Warren Lee
Gors, *Century Magazine*, vol. 32, May 1886, p. 136; and for
the illustration, "Rush's Lancers — the 6th Pennsylvania
Cavalry," *Battles and Leaders of the Civil War*, New York,
1887, vol. 2, p. 319

Signed at the lower left with brush: *HOMER*; inscribed by
the artist on verso: *April 2nd / The 6th Penn Cavalr . . . /
Embarking at Alexandr . . . / April 2 for Old Point Comfort /
This is a full Regt. All the men have / Lances which they
use with great ski . . . / This being the only Regt. of the kind
in the Serv . . . / I thought you would like it / H.*

Pencil, gray wash; 8⅝ x 15⅞

(219 x 403)

Losses in right and left margins

1912-12-137

5.

ARMY ENCAMPMENT

Verso: Various sketches and notations, with the date *April 5*
1862
Several of the figures were used in the painting, *In Front
of Yorktown, 1862,* Yale University Gallery of Fine Arts;
and in the illustration, "61st Regiment in Camp," *Battles
and Leaders of the Civil War,* New York, 1887, vol. 2, p. 195

Pencil; 11¾ x 24¼
(298 x 625)
1912-12-138

6.
MARCHING INFANTRY COLUMN
Probably 1862
Pencil, charcoal, white gouache; 13¼ x 20⅛
(336 x 513)
1912-12-204A

7.

SOLDIERS DRILLING

1862-1864
Study for the illustration, "Feeling the Enemy," *Battles
and Leaders of the Civil War*, New York, 1887, vol. 3, p. 224
Black and white chalk on light brown paper; 10⅞ x
15⅜ (275 x 388)
1912-12-104

8.

THE WALKING WOUNDED

1861-1862

Pen and brown ink; $4^{13}/_{16}$ x $7^{9}/_{16}$ (122 x 191)

1912-12-121

9.

ARMY WAGON AND MULE

    About 1862
    Pencil, gray wash on blue paper; 5⅛ x 8⁹⁄₁₆
    (131 x 217)
    1912-12-150

10.

FOUR STUDIES OF SOLDIERS' HEADS
Verso: Various sketches and color notations
1862-1863
Homer referred to the sheet several times: for the painting, *Officers at Camp Benton, Maryland*, Boston Public Library; for the wood engravings, "Pay Day in the Army of the Potomac" and "Home from the War," *Harper's Weekly*, February 28 and June 13, 1863; and for the lithographed postcard, "Building Castles," no. 1 in the series, *Life in Camp*, part 1
Inscribed by the artist with color notations
Black chalk on light brown paper; 16¹⁵/₁₆ x 9⅞
(429 x 250)
1912-12-102

11.
CAVALRY OFFICER'S BOOTS
Verso: Supine man
1862-1866
Study for the painting, *Prisoners from the Front,*
Metropolitan Museum of Art
Inscribed by the artist in pencil near left boot: *high light*
Pencil; 6¹¹⁄₁₆ x 4¹³⁄₁₆ (174 x 121)
1912-12-113

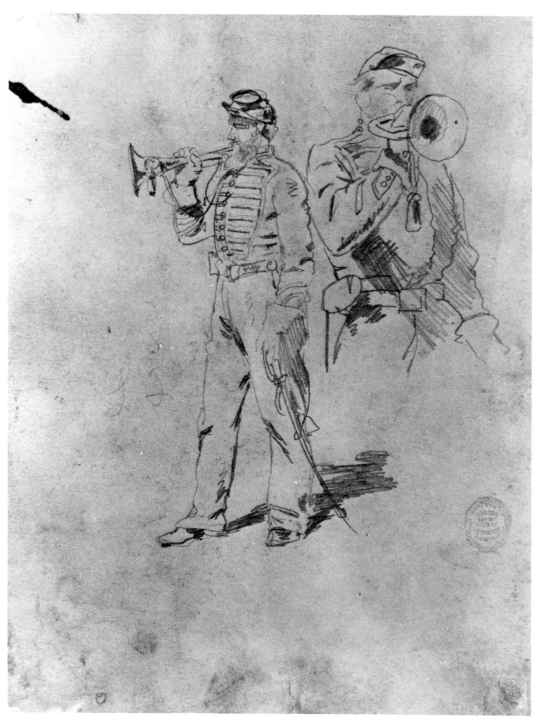

12.
TWO STUDIES OF A BUGLER
Verso: An army camp
1862-1864
Possibly a study for the wood
  engraving, "1860-1870,"
Harper's Weekly, January 8, 1870
Pencil; 9 x 6¾ (228 x 172)
1912-12-115

13.

CAVALRY SOLDIER
1863
Signed with initials and dated in pencil at lower right:
WH / 1863
Black chalk on brown paper; 14¼ x 7¹⁵⁄₁₆ (361 x 201)
1912-12-106

14.
CAVALRY SOLDIER
1863
Black chalk on brown paper;
14⅜ x 9½ (366 x 241)
1912-12-107

15.
STUDIES OF SOLDIERS
1863-1864
The figure at the lower left was used in
the illustration, ''The Baggage Guard,''
The Century Magazine, vol. 35, 1887-1888, p. 324;
the figure at the upper left in the illustration,
''Feeling the Enemy,'' *Battles and Leaders of
the Civil War*, New York, 1887, vol. 3, p. 224
Black and white chalk on brown paper; 24¹/₁₆ x 16⅛
(625 x 407). The sheet has been cut and rejoined.
1912-12-101

16.
SOLDIER LOADING A RIFLE
Verso: Various studies of soldiers
1863-1864
Study for the illustration, "Feeling
the Enemy," *Battles and Leaders
of the Civil War*, New York, 1887,
vol. 3, p. 224
Black chalk, with corrections in
white gouache; 16⅞ x 12¹⁵/₁₆
(428 x 328)
1912-12-99

17.
YOUNG SOLDIER; SEPARATE STUDY OF A
SOLDIER GIVING WATER TO A WOUNDED
COMPANION

1861-1864
The young soldier appears in the wood engraving, "A Bivouac
Fire on the Potomac," *Harper's Weekly*, December 21, 1861
Oil sketch, pencil on canvas; 14³/₁₆ x 7³/₁₆ (360 x 182)
1912-12-110

18.

WOUNDED SOLDIER BEING GIVEN A DRINK
FROM A CANTEEN
    Verso: Drill ground
    1864
    Signed and dated in charcoal at lower left: *HOMER 1864*
    Charcoal, white chalk on green paper; 14⅜ x 19½ (365 x 500)
    1912-12-100

19.

DRUMMER, SEEN FROM THE BACK

Verso: Studies of soldiers in action
Probably 1864
Study for the illustration, ''Beating the Long Roll,''
Battles and Leaders of the Civil War, New York,
1887, vol. 4, p. 179
Charcoal, white chalk on blue-green paper;
16⅞ x 11⅜
(427 x 288)
1912-12-108

20.

ZOUAVE

1864

Study for the painting, *Pitching Quoits*, Fogg Art Museum, Harvard University

Signed with initials and dated in black chalk at lower left: *W. H. / 1864*

Black and white chalk on blue-green paper; 16⅞ x 7½ (428 x 190)

1912-12-109

1912-12-131

21.
TWO STUDIES OF A YOUNG GIRL LOOKING
OVER HER SHOULDER
 Verso: Drill ground, inscribed *Camp Winfield Scott*
 About 1862
 Study for the wood engraving, "Cutting a Figure,"
 Every Saturday, February 4, 1871
 Pencil on brown paper; 12⅞ x 6¼ (326 x 158)
 1912-12-131

22.
MAN WITH A SCYTHE
    About 1865
    Study for the painting, *A Veteran in a New Field,*
    Metropolitan Museum of Art; and for the wood engraving,
    "Making Hay," *Harper's Weekly,* July 6, 1872
    Pencil, with corrections in white gouache; 5⁹/₁₆ x 14¹/₁₆
    (142 x 357)
    1912-12-258

23.
VIEW OF PARIS

1867
Probably a study for the painting, *Gargoyles of Notre Dame*,
James M. Thomson Collection
Signed with initials and dated in pencil at upper right:
WH Paris 1867
Pen and brown ink, pencil on brown paper; 7³/₁₆ x 11⅛
(182 x 282)
1912-12-58

24.

INTERNATIONAL TEA PARTY
About 1867
Pencil, black and gray wash; 8¹/₁₆ x 10⁵/₁₆
(204 x 262)
1912-12-269

25.

ARTISTS SKETCHING IN THE WHITE MOUNTAINS

Verso: Various sketches of male heads
1868
Study for the painting, *Artists Sketching in the White
Mountains*, Mr. and Mrs. Charles Payson Collection; and
for the wood engraving, "The Artist in the Country,"
Appleton's Journal, June 19, 1868
Inscribed by the artist with color notations

Pencil, blackened on verso for transfer; 8⁵⁄₁₆ x 5¹³⁄₁₆
(211 x 147)
1912-12-263

26.

BRIDLE PATH, WHITE MOUNTAINS

1868

Study for the paintings, *Bridle Path, White Mountains*,
Sterling and Francine Clark Art Institute, Williamstown,
and *Mt. Washington*, Art Institute of Chicago; and for
the wood engraving, "Summit of Mt. Washington,"
Harper's Weekly, July 10, 1869

Inscribed by the artist in pencil at lower right:
Mt. Washington / Aug. 1868
Pencil; 6¾ x 9⅝ (171 x 243)
1912-12-221

27.

SUMMIT OF MT. WASHINGTON

1869
Study for the painting, *Mt. Washington*, Art Institute of
Chicago; and for the wood engraving, "Summit of
Mt. Washington," *Harper's Weekly*, July 10, 1869
Signed and dated in pencil at lower right: Mt. Washington/
Homer 1869
Pencil; 5⅛ x 9¾ (131 x 248)
1912-12-127

28.
HORSES AND WAGON (The Picnic Excursion)
Verso: Group around a fireside
1868
Study for the wood engravings, "The Picnic Excursion,"
Appleton's Journal, August 14, 1869, and "The Last Days
of Harvest," *Harper's Weekly,* December 6, 1873
Pencil; 4 x 6 (102 x 151)
1912-12-260

29.

MOUNTAIN CLIMBER RESTING

1868-1869
Study for the painting, *A Mountain Climber Resting*,
Paul Peralta-Ramos Collection; and for the wood engraving,
"The Coolest Spot in New England—Summit of Mount
Washington," *Harper's Bazar* [sic], July 23, 1870
Black and white crayon, blackened on verso for transfer,
on brown paper; 7¾ x 13¹⁵⁄₁₆ (197 x 353)
1912-12-98

30.
GIRL HOLDING A DRINKING GLASS
Probably 1869
Study for the wood engraving, "On the Beach at Long
Branch," *Appleton's Journal,* August 21, 1869
Black and white chalk; 12⅝ x 5⅝ (320 x 143)
1912-12-75

31.
SNAP THE WHIP
   Verso: Young girl in a sunbonnet
   Probably 1872
   Study for the paintings, *Snap the Whip*, Metropolitan
   Museum of Art, and Butler Art Institute, Youngstown; and
   for the wood engraving, "Snap the Whip," *Harper's*
   Weekly, September 20, 1873

Black and white chalk on green paper; 9³/₁₆ x 16½
(235 x 420)
1912-12-82

32.

GIRL WITH APPLE TREE

1870s

Pencil; 7¹¹/₁₆ x 5⁹/₁₆ (196 x 142)

1912-12-70

33.

TWO GIRLS UNDER A TREE

1870s

Pencil; 8³/₁₆ x 4¹⁵/₁₆ (207 x 126)

1912-12-77

34.
SHEEP RESTING
Verso: Figures in a landscape
1878
Study for the watercolors, *Shepherdess under the Trees*,
private collection, and *Shepherdess of Houghton Farm*,
Sterling and Francine Clark Art Institute, Williamstown
Signed and dated with brush at lower left:
HOMER Oct 15th 1878

Pencil, watercolor; 8⅞ x 11¼ (225 x 286)
1912-12-55

35.

WAVERLY OAKS

1875-1878

Study for the watercolor, *Waverly Oaks,* Mrs. Thomas
Card Collection

Signed in pencil at lower right: *HOMER;* inscribed on
verso in pencil: *Waverly Oaks / $10;* in pen and
brown ink, *No. 14*

Pencil, white gouache on brown paper; 5¹³⁄₁₆ x 8¹⁄₁₆
(148 x 204)
1912-12-87

36.
TWO YOUNG GIRLS
  1878-1879
  Signed in white gouache at lower left: *HOMER*
  Brown chalk, white gouache on brown paper;
  10⅜ x 7⅜ (263 x 187)
  1912-12-276

37.

YOUNG WOMAN CARRYING A BASKET
1879
Signed and dated in pencil at lower right:
HOMER / 1879
Pencil; 12³/₁₆ x 7¾ (309 x 198)
1916-15-1
Gift of Charles W. Gould

38.
SHEPHERDESS RESTING
1878-1880
Charcoal; 14¼ x 22 (362 x 560)
1912-12-206

39.
SEATED GIRL
1878-1880
Study for the watercolor, *Girl on a Wall*,
private collection
Signed in black chalk at lower left: *HOMER*
Black chalk, gray wash, white gouache
on light brown paper; 19¾ x 14 (502 x 357)
1912-12-274

40.
YOUNG GIRL WITH A BASKET, SEATED
1878-1880
Signed in pencil at lower right: *Winslow Homer*
Black chalk, white gouache on gray paper; 15⅞ x 10³⁄₁₆
(403 x 259)
1912-12-79

41.

GIRL HOLDING A SHELL
1879
Signed with initials and dated in charcoal at
lower right: *WH / 1879*
Charcoal; 12$\frac{7}{16}$ x 8 (315 x 204)
1912-12-275

42.

TWO GIRLS IN A FIELD

1879
Study for an illustration in *Hours with Art and Artists*
by George W. Sheldon, New York, 1882, p. 136
Signed and dated in pencil at lower right:
Winslow Homer / 1879; inscribed across lower margin:

Copyright given to D. Appleton and Co.: at left margin:
9251 1 Jan 13 XXX / 5" high; on verso: *No. 19 / $25*
Pencil; 9⁵/₁₆ x 9¹⁵/₁₆ (237 x 253)
1912-12-80

43.
TWO GIRLS
1879
Carbon tracing, retouched; 7⁷⁄₁₆ x 4⅜ (189 x 112)
1912-12-71

44.
GIRL WITH A LUNCH PAIL
1879
Carbon tracing, retouched; 8⁵⁄₁₆ x 4³⁄₁₆ (211 x 107)
1912-12-72

45.

GIRL SEATED ON A PORCH STEP
    1879
    Pencil; $6^{11}/_{16}$ x $5^{9}/_{16}$ (169 x 142)
    1912-12-78

46.
BOY ON A SWING
1879
Signed with initial and dated in pencil
at lower left: *H 79*
Pencil; 10¼ x 8⁷⁄₁₆ (260 x 214)
1912-12-65

47.
BOY AND GIRL IN A ROWBOAT
1876-1880
Possibly a study for the painting, *Gloucester Harbor*,
Carleton Mitchell Collection
Pencil, gray wash; 10 x 14 (253 x 355)
1912-12-222

48.

TWO GIRLS IN A ROWBOAT

1876-1880
Pencil, watercolor; 9⁹/₁₆ x 13 (243 x 330)
1912-12-223

49.
FOUR ROWBOATS WITH CHILDREN
1880s
Pencil, watercolor; 9¾ x 13⅝ (247 x 347)
1912-12-13

50.

SCHOONER NEAR A ROCKY COAST
    About 1880
    Pencil; 4¾ x 7⅝ (122 x 194)
    1912-12-3

51.

TWO SCHOONERS AND DORIES

About 1880
Pencil on light brown paper; 5¾ x 13¾ (146 x 350)
1912-12-5

52.

SCHOONER WITH THREE DORIES

1880

Signed and dated in pencil at lower right:

Winslow Homer 1880

Pencil, white gouache on light brown paper; 5⅛ x 9⅜

(130 x 238)

1912-12-12

53.

FISHERMEN AND WOMEN STOWING NETS IN A BEACHED DORY

1881
Pencil, white gouache on light gray paper (two sheets
joined, overlapping); 7¼ x 14⁵⁄₁₆ (184 x 363)
1912-12-20

54.

BAY AT TYNEMOUTH, ENGLAND
1881
Charcoal, white chalk; 13½ x 21¹⁵⁄₁₆ (343 x 557)
1912-12-84

55.

FISHERMEN BEACHING A BOAT

1881
Signed and dated in charcoal at lower right: *HOMER '81*
Charcoal, white gouache; 6⅝ x 12¼ (168 x 311)
1912-12-40

56.

FISHERMEN BEACHING A DORY

1881

Signed in charcoal at lower left: *HOMER*

Charcoal, white chalk; 7 x 11¹³⁄₁₆ (177 x 300)

1912-12-41

57.
TWO WOMEN AND A CHILD AT A RAIL,
OVERLOOKING THE BEACH AT TYNEMOUTH
1881
Signed in charcoal at lower left: *HOMER*
Charcoal; 8⅜ x 11¾ (213 x 297)
1912-12-17

58.

FISHERMEN IN OILSKINS, TYNEMOUTH
1881
Study for the painting, *Fishermen Watching a Storm*,
David Gray Collection; and for the watercolor,
The Life Brigade, Mrs. Philip Stockton Collection
Charcoal, white chalk; 14¾ x 12¹/₁₆ (374 x 306)
1912-12-25

59.

THE LIFE BOAT (The Wreck of the "Iron Crown")

1881
Study for the watercolor, *The Wreck of the "Iron Crown,"*
Carleton Mitchell Collection
Signed with black chalk at lower left: *HOMER,*
partially obliterated inscription at lower margin with
the date *1881;* numbered *27* on verso

Black chalk, black wash, white gouache; 13⅞ x 19¹⁄₁₆
(354 x 484)
1912-12-130

60.
THE LIFE LINE
1882-1883
Study for the painting, *The Life Line*,
Philadelphia Museum of Art;
and for the etchings, *The Life Line*, and *Saved*
Inscribed by the artist in black chalk
at lower left: *The Life Line / First Sketch*
Black and white chalk; 17½ x 11 (445 x 280)
1912-12-34

61.
THE HERRING NET
1884-1885
Study for the painting, *The Herring Net*, The Art
Institute of Chicago
Numbered in black chalk on verso: *60*
Black, brown, and white chalk on green paper; 16⅝ x 20⅝
(422 x 523)
1916-15-2
Gift of Charles W. Gould

62.
SHIP DECK WITH TWO WOMEN LASHED TO THE MAST
1886
Partially illegible inscription by the artist in charcoal at
lower margin: *Hell . . . July . . . '86*
Charcoal, white gouache on brown cardboard;
12³⁄₁₆ x 16³⁄₁₆ (309 x 410)
1912-12-35

63.

HARD-A-PORT

1885-1890
Inscribed by the artist in charcoal at lower margin:
Hard-a-port
Charcoal; 12⅛ x 19½ (307 x 497)
1912-12-42

64.
SEASCAPE, PROUT'S NECK
   About 1890
   Charcoal; 17⁷/₁₆ x 23 (442 x 587)
   1912-12-85

65.

STORM COMING (Shore with Clouded Sky)
About 1890
Signed in black chalk at lower left: *HOMER*; inscribed
by the artist on verso: *Thund . . .*, and numbered 75
Black chalk; 15⅝ x 22¹/₁₆ (396 x 561)
1912-12-198

66.

SEACOAST WITH SCRUB PINES, PROUT'S NECK, EASTERN POINT
    1885-1890
    Probably a study for the paintings, *Coast in Winter,*
    Worcester Art Museum, and *Winter Coast,* Philadelphia
    Museum of Art
    Charcoal, white chalk on gray paper; 18 x 23⅞
    (459 x 616)
    1912-12-187

67.

BLACK POINT, SCARBOROUGH (Rocky Shore with Surf)

1885-1890
Probably a study for the painting, *Coast in Winter*,
Worchester Art Museum
Numbered on verso: *52*
Charcoal, white chalk on gray paper; 15¼ x 23⁹⁄₁₆
(390 x 600)
1912-12-188

68.
TREE ROOTS, PROUT'S NECK
    About 1885
    Signed in charcoal at lower left: *HOMER*
    Numbered on verso: *50e*
    Charcoal, white chalk on gray paper; 15⅝ x 22⅞
    (395 x 580)
    1912-12-90

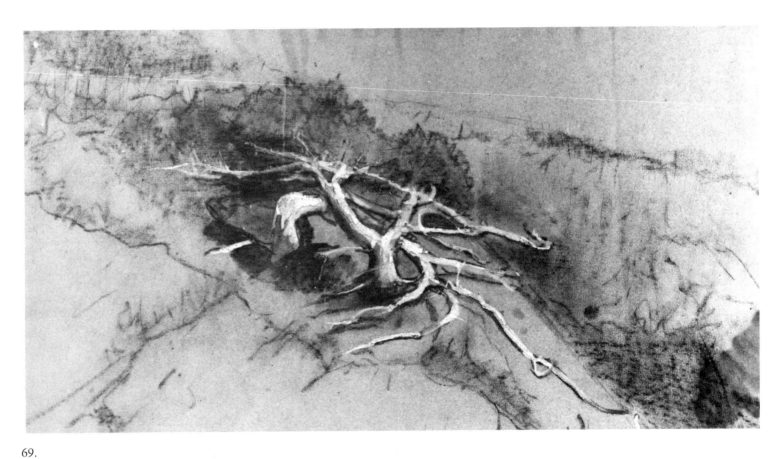

69.
TREE ROOTS ON A HILLSIDE, PROUT'S NECK
    About 1885
    Study for the painting, *Coast of Maine,* The Art Institute
    of Chicago
    Numbered on verso: *37*
    Charcoal, white gouache on gray paper; 11¹¹/₁₆ x 23¼
    (298 x 592)
    1912-12-91

70.
TWO-MASTED SCHOONER,
WITH DORY
1894
Signed with brush and red wash at
lower right: *HOMER 1894*
Watercolor; 21½ x 15⅛ (546 x 383)
1912-12-189

71.
THE SIGNAL OF DISTRES
About 1890
Study for the painting,
The Signal of Distress,
Mr. and Mrs. Cornelius
Vanderbilt Whitney
Collection
Watercolor, pencil;
13⅞ x 11⅝ (353 x 295)
1912-12-43

72.
THE LOOKOUT;
SEPARATE STUDY OF A SAILOR
WITH RAISED ARM
 1895-1896
 Study for the painting, *The Lookout—
 All's Well*, Museum of Fine
 Arts, Boston; *Sailor with Raised Arm*
 probably a study for *The Wreck*,
 Carnegie Institute, Pittsburgh
 Various notations at upper margin
 Charcoal, white gouache; 13¾ x 10⁵⁄₁₆
 (348 x 262)
 1912-12-33

73.

THE LOOKOUT

1895-1896

Possibly a study for the painting, *The Lookout — All's Well*,
Museum of Fine Arts, Boston
Illegible inscription in pen and black ink with the numbers
102 / L 15 at upper right; inscribed by the artist in
pencil on verso: *Taking a bath / will open
up as soon / as possible / W H / Sunday*

Black crayon, with corrections in white gouache on
cardboard; 12⁷/₁₆ x 13¹³/₁₆ (316 x 315)
1912-12-32

74.

LANDSCAPE IN MORNING HAZE, DEER AT A FENCE
   About 1892
   Watercolor, pencil; 14½ x 21 (368 x 535)
   1913-18-3

75.

MOUNTAIN RIVER (Mountain Lake)
    About 1895
    Black chalk, pencil, gray, blue, and black wash; 14 x 20⅞
    (355 x 533)
    1913-18-4

76.

FISHERMAN IN QUEBEC (Fisherman in the Adirondacks)
    About 1895
    Signed with initials in black wash at lower right: *W.H.* —
    Pencil, black and gray wash, white gouache on gray paper;
    12¹/₁₆ x 19¹⁵/₁₆ (306 x 509)
    1912-12-89

77.
VALLEY AND HILLSIDE
1890-1895
Watercolor, pencil; 14 x 20 (354 x 509)
1912-12-185

78.

DECK PASSENGERS

1880-1885

Watercolor, pencil; 8³⁄₁₆ x 13¹⁄₁₆ (209 x 332)

1912-12-57

79.

CUBAN HILLSIDE

1885

Signed and dated in pencil at lower left: *Winslow Homer 1885*

Pencil, white chalk, white gouache on gray paper;

$10^{13}/_{16}$ x $17^{7}/_{16}$ (299 x 442)

1912-12-93

80.
ROYAL PALM, CUBA
1885
Signed in pencil at lower right: *Winslow Homer / Royal Palm*
Pencil, white chalk on gray paper; $11^{15}/_{16}$ x $17^{11}/_{16}$ (302 x 448)
1912-12-94

81.
HILLSIDE WITH CLUMPS OF MAGUEY
1899
Watercolor, pencil; 14½ x 9⅛ (368 x 232)
1912-12-92

82.
THE GULF STREAM
1898-1899
Study for the painting, *The Gulf Stream*, Metropolitan Museum of Art, and related to the watercolors, *Derelict and Sharks*, Mrs. Ian MacDonald Collection, and *The Gulf Stream*, The Art Institute of Chicago
Watercolor; 14½ x 10¹/₁₆ (368 x 256)
1912-12-36

Oils

83.
FRENCH FARMYARD
18⅛ x 14½ (460 x 365)
1917-14-9

84.
MAN WITH A SCYTHE
17⅛ x 22 (434 x 560)
1918-20-10

85.
FISHERMEN AT SUNDOWN
  Signed at lower right: *HOMER*
  12½ x 21¼ (313 x 540)
  1915-17-1

86.
SANDY BEACH WITH BREAKERS
   10¼ x 21¾ (260 x 551)
   1918-20-8

87.

MOUNTAIN WAGON

Signed and dated at lower right: *WINSLOW HOMER 1869(?)*
11¾ x 15¾ (299 x 402)
1918-20-9

88.

SUNLIGHT AND SHADOW
  Signed at lower right: *HOMER*
  15¾ x 22½ (402 x 576)
  1917-14-7

89.
THE BUTTERFLY
Signed and dated at lower right: *Winslow HOMER 1872*
15½ x 22¾ (396 x 578)
1917-14-1

90.
SUMMER AFTERNOON
22½ x 15½ (571 x 396)
1917-14-5

91.
A COUNTRY LAD
Signed and dated at right, on fence:
HOMER 1873
22½ x 15½ (574 x 393)
1917-14-2

92.

GIRL SHELLING PEAS

    Signed at lower left: *WINSLOW HOMER*

    12¼ x 17¼ (311 x 436)

    1918-20-12

93.

AUTUMN TREETOPS

Signed and dated at lower left: *Homer Oct. 11, 1873*
13½ x 20 (345 x 508)
1918-20-2

94.
GATHERING AUTUMN LEAVES
38¼ x 24¼ (970 x 618)
1917-14-3

95.

MAN WITH A KNAPSACK

Signed and dated at lower right:
Winslow Homer Oct. 10, 1873
15¼ x 22¼ (387 x 569)
1918-20-1

96.

FARMYARD WITH DUCK AND CHICKENS
Signed at lower left: *HOMER*
15¼ x 22½ (390 x 574)
1918-20-4

97.
HAYSTACKS AND CHILDREN
Signed and dated at lower left: *HOMER 1874*
15½ x 22½ (392 x 574)
1918-20-3

98.
THE WATERMELON BOYS
    Signed and dated at lower left: *HOMER 1876*
    24⅛ x 38⅛ (613 x 968)
    1917-14-6

99.
BOY AND GIRL IN A FIELD WITH SHEEP
15½ x 22½ (392 x 573)
1918-20-6

100.
TWO GIRLS WITH SUNBONNETS IN A FIELD
15¾ x 22½ (397 x 572)
1918-20-5

101.
THE BEAN PICKER
 Signed and dated at lower left:
 Winslow Homer 1878
 22½ x 15½ (571 x 393)
 1917-14-8

102.
THE YELLOW JACKET
Signed and dated at lower left: *HOMER 1879*
22¾ x 15½ (578 x 397)
1917-14-4

103.
GARRISON HOUSE, YORK, MAINE
    15¾ x 22½ (398 x 573)
    1918-20-11

104.
GIRL PICKING APPLE BLOSSOMS
Signed and dated at lower right: *HOMER 1879*
15¾ x 22¾ (400 x 578)
1918-20-7

Etching

105.

SAVED

Signed on the plate at lower right: *Winslow Homer fe.*
22¾ x 32⅝ (577 x 830)
1949-70-1
Purchased in memory of Erskine Hewitt

Wood Engraving

106.

SNAP THE WHIP

    Signed on the block: *HOMER 1873*
    13½ x 20½ (344 x 522)
    1947-4-60
    Gift of John Goldsmith Phillips, Jr.

INDEX OF TITLES

Prints

Oil Paintings